Fragrance of the Heart

ALICIA BUDHRAM

ISBN: 978-0-578-61608-7

Editor: Sharp Editorial, LLC
Website: www.sharpeditorial.com

Cover design/graphics:
Pavankumar Kumkarran

Author: Alicia Budhram
https://www.infinitecreativityaliciabudhram.com

Publisher: Marla Lafayette
Un-Filtered Publications
Website: www.unfilteredpublications.com

Love Languages

Prem प्रेम

Aí 爱

Eros

Amore

Liebe

प्रेम

L'amour

ప్రేమ Prēma

Priya प्रिय

Grá

사랑 salang

Pasada hai

Prīti

liebe

Aşk

lyublyu

yêu

Kātal காதல்

mohabbat

miłość

hkyithkyinnmayttar

Heart Languages

Itayam

hRdaya

Cœur

Corazón

Herz

Xīn

dil

Croí

Shinzō

Cuore

καρδιά

Coração

Guṇḍe

Сердце serdtse

Kalp

simjang

Khwāmrạk

snēhaṁ

Anpu

DEDICATION

This book is dedicated to the gem of individuals who have been a monumental part of my journey, development, and growth and who have cheered me on continuously and consistently. My love, gratitude, and highest regards.

My vibrations of appreciation to the Universe in her wisdom. When I'm in alignment with her, my creativity is unmatched.

ACKNOWLEDGMENTS

Dolly, 1,000,000 thank yous for your beautiful soul, understanding, and insights.

Shardz, Laci, and Marla, and to the One who also wishes that I write poetry continuously, you know who you are, thank you to the universe for bringing us together and for your faith in me.

A nomad, searching, directionless,
Seeking refuge from this drought.
My roses withered under the sun of sadness.
This summer of my heart is endless.

Parched and barren, the days stretch on.
Laying breathlessly on the ground,
This arid heart prays for a shower;
Silently, not making a sound.

Beseeching the gods to blow the wind
Thy fragrance in my direction,
To drench this dry heart with thy love,
This be my heart's confession.

Extend now thy hand to me.
Fuse me back with thy refreshing love.
Come with storms and heavy rains.
Pour unceasingly from above.

Table of Contents

1

STONE HEARTS

Oh, hearts that have turned to stone,
Unable to feel a thing,
The warmth of love allows to melt
The stone hearts that you bring.

Fond of safety you have been,
Afraid to open its doors
After a tragic story
Of a few promises broken.

That healing rhythm,
Searing stones, reclaiming homes,
Carrying ancient wisdom,
From heart to heart, it roams.

Filling hearts with hope,
Resuscitating after devastation;
Be not afraid
To trust this magical potion.

2

FREEDOM

Neither ownership nor possession I seek of you.
A bird in a gilded cage, you'd be if I do,
Fluttering about with clipped wings
Or a puppet hanging on multiple strings.

Dance not to the beat of my drum;
In loving, there is freedom.

If I restrict or restrain your flight
Or hold on to you a bit too tight,
Impinge with what I desire for you,
I hope you'd know just what to do.

Dance not to the beat of my drum;
In loving, there is freedom.

A caged creature, for its counterpart longs
The boundless sky where it belongs;
Ideas of how our love should be
Will hold us back from flying free.

Dance not, we shouldn't to each other's drum;
In loving, there is freedom.

In my presence, experience liberties.
Sail through the sky of possibilities.
Fly beside me, undefined,
And wherever you go, I'm somewhere behind.

3

SECRETS

I am the name upon your soul,
The radiance in your sight,
The coffee that energizes you,
The blanket over you at night.

I am the curve in your smile,
The forgotten right-side sock,
The bird you admire from afar,
Perched upon a rock.

The pounding rhythm of your heart,
Your roof against the cold,
I am a secret on time's wings
For centuries gone untold.

4

ENCHANTER

I scuttled from the fire, frazzled,
Safe in my retreat.
You flowed like a breeze towards me,
Sweeping me off my feet.

A tour of the cosmos
Off into the inky night,
Lifting me effortlessly
As would an avatar of might.

Earth was a pea-sized bubble.
So very small was it,
From here upon the stars
That had awaited our visit.

On the edge of a sparkling cluster,
Awed by your mysterious charm,
I had been basking
When I should've raised an alarm.

Your scent was a heady drug.
Your form was quite a sight.
I did not regret trusting you,
Mysterious enchanter of the night.

5

MINE ALONE

I never asked your name.
I did not need to know.
In the dark, I knew your contours.
Every inch, a reverent delight.

The darkness shrouded you
In absolute alluring mystery.
I liked it that way.
You belonged to me by night.

I owned you for that time.
You were mine alone.
We never said any words,
Never felt the need.

Silence was the known language.
A shy, inaudible whisper,
A pounding heart, the call;
To my beckon, did you pay attention?

Your eyes - sparkling stars,
Burning into mine;
Time - pointlessly infinite,
I caved, involuntarily.

You were all I ever wanted,
Especially in the dark
When you were mine alone,
If only momentarily.

6

CALLING

The heart resonates
In silent reverie,
Messages sent to the universe
Through a vibrating frequency.

In solitude, you, too, are found,
Staring at the moon,
Tuned into the roaring ocean,
Promising our meeting soon.

Tranquil, your heart shall recognize
A fraction of a jolted motion,
Way above all distant sounds,
Like that of the ebullient ocean.

The nudge of your resonating answer,
Rhythmic pulsing beats,
Continents separates the physicality
Where the moon and the ocean meet.

7

TIMELESS

Footprints stamped on the sands of time,
The winds dare not erase.
For a sign that I had been here,
I leave behind a memory's trace.

Trudging the burning desert,
Searching amidst the grains of sand,
Why have you etched your face upon my heart?
Will I this torture withstand?

For the cool shade of your shadow,
I desperately thirst
To shelter me from this blazing heat.
Let me, in your piercing gaze, immerse.

Your face reflected in the sea of sand.
I ran gleefully, arms outstretched,
Anticipating your cool embrace,
Your form before me, once far-fetched.

To my horror, you were not there.
Your image was a reflection of my desperate heart,
A mirage born of my heart's longing.
Timelessly, in my heart, you remain.

8

CHOICE

Distinctly in her silent domain,
The room is her private space.
Her gaze will burn your insides
With a piercing straight face.

Through the windows of her eyes,
Actions she perceives.
Her decisions stemming from past events
To wear her heart hidden or on her sleeve.

Though her body you touched,
Her heart you never did.
She decides when that happens,
But you'd hope she does and let open her lid.

In the silent space of her domain,
She chooses secrets to share,
Or in a spell, she struts away;
You'd really want to beware.

It is always her call
To allow you in her private space,
To keep her walls up,
Or allow her heart to race.

9

THE HEART'S CALLING

When the heart invitingly calls,
Will I run unhesitant in response?
Will I heed without a moment's pause
And willingly give in to what it wants?

For I have been a seed, dormant;
The darkness, warm and private.
There I waited, patiently.
Waiting, I wasn't fond of it.

Your call came, a strong, poignant feeling.
I jolted in shock.
There, on my heart's door, where it's ever quiet,
Was now a gentle knock.

Should I throw caution to the wind
And send a reply?
Should I, in this moment,
My feelings, deny?

Should I allow the doors of my heart to open,
Beckoning love's scent to enter in?
Should I bow defeated and let love win?

10

WELL

A bubbling well you were.
I, the bucket,
Dipping into your depths endlessly.

Willing your water,
"Quench this unending thirst,"
I beckoned breathlessly.

I gulped.
I was parched.
Someone whispered gently.

I spun around,
Horrified at the words,
"Dearest one, do drink slowly!"

Inhaling deeply,
I sank to the ground,
Skeptical of that voice.

I attempted to stand.
My legs wouldn't allow.
I couldn't keep my poise.

'Twas so long ago.
Memories are now faded.
Perhaps I was hallucinating.

Dehydrated, light-headed I was.
Searching, hoping...
The trek was tiring.

A sip I yearn
From your timeless oasis.
It has been an arduous journey.

For the cool shelters of your shades,
And that refreshing feeling
Of dipping in your depths endlessly

11

UGLY TRUTHS

Ugly truths, seven ounces,
Bottled as a potion sold,
Leaving one in a drunken stupor;
Oh, what lies of love have we told!

This bewitching miracle elixir
is craved neurotically,
Dying for just a drop of this quencher
That leaves a bitter aftertaste.

At the tip of our tongues,
For but a brief moment,
We hadn't had our fill;
Our hearts still ringing in torment.

It's been a long season of fables,
A season of ugly truths,
A season of fleetingly emotions,
A season of vain pursuits.

Centuries of myths,
Aeon of fables,
Years of suffocating phobic lies,
Lifetimes of yearning for authenticity.

12

TIME

What is present I enjoy
In the here and now;
May I be found with no regrets
A future second from now.

For the past to relive
Or the future to arrive,
Neither do I yearn.
In the now is the thrill of being alive.

In this moment, I am fully consumed.
Every cell vibrates life,
Bursting with passion,
Breathing, existing.

Experiences shape my future,
all created in the now;
The present moment,
This moment only, I will fully allow.

In the now, I am who I am.
I am all I will ever be.
Time exists only now
In this very moment for me.

13

ENCHANTER

When I entered your cottage,
It was dark. I was soaking wet,
Dripping and shivering.
I hadn't seen you yet.

Lamps were dimmed,
Your form barely visible,
Save for the sparkle in your eyes.
To stay calm was a task not possible.

You took me to a room.
I was made to sit;
Brought a steamy cup of tea
I was asked to sip.

You dried my hair.
I was drenched, shivering.
The sound of my pounding heart,
Loud above your whispering.

Lifting my arms, you whispered, "Stand,"
While removing layers of clothing.
The sound of my pounding heart,
Loud above your whispering.

My shy gaze rose. I met yours
As the last piece stood between us.
Never was there hesitancy.
I did not make a fuss.

Your eyes were blazing emerald.
Raging, they burned into mine.
Was it that tea I had,
Or a special spell-binding wine?

I clutched your arms,
Supporting my failing knees.
Never had I experienced this,
Never emotions such as these.

I cannot forget that fervent look,
Never that night we met.
It must've been some weird spell pulling me
Into your bewitching net.

14

YOUR GAZE

Searching eyes, scaling trains and planes
At stop lights.
Nowhere were you to be found.
My heart understood not.

Searching in vain,
Seeking within every eye,
Your gaze I knew I'd recognize
And your heart's distinctive rhythm.

Our eyes tell stories of
A meeting long ago.
Carving your name upon on my soul,
I drowned in your fathomless depths.

Time existed not;
We stood on a frozen globe,
Fingers entwined,
Hearts somersaulting in our chests.

In a blink of staring,
We are meeting again.
Standing on the edge of a piercing soul-search,
You simply smiled and walked away.

I lost movement as I stared,
Watching you strut off, helplessly,
But you were meant to be here, my heart protested;
You were meant to stay.

Hoarsely whispered, voice failing,
Footsteps fading,
The sound of two hearts breaking
And yearning mixed with the pouring rain.

Searching once more, trains and planes
At stop lights,
My heart quietly consoled,
"You'll definitely meet him again."

15

LOVE DEFINED

Your love is gentle; the stirring wind
Whispering across my face
And the happy, golden sunshine
Arriving in his own pace.

Your touch is the drenching coolness
Of the sweet awakening dawn
And the first sign of autumn
After a winter's night long gone.

Your smile is the comfort I always need,
Like a Band-Aid on a wounded knee.
Your giggles dance their way to my heart,
Ringing across healingly.

Your sight calms my raging thoughts.
Your gentleness soothes my tired mind.
Your glances set fire to my freezing soul.
You, dearest one, are truly love-defined.

16

TALES

Unchanged remains the plot;
To love, to gain,
To lose, to fail.

Ever-changing lines
Paint the pages of life
Telling just this tale.

Laughter and sobs
Intermittingly;
What's the Earth without the rain?

A barren, thirsty land,
So the wins don't come
Without the pain.

What's a heart without love?
An Atlantis, distant,
A ship without a sail.

Ever-changing lines
Paint the pages of life
Telling just this tale.

17

WAVES

Gently winding, unhurriedly,
Washing away all uncertainty,
Splashing random imaginings
Of brand new beginnings.

Rumbling to the surface, unceasingly,
Your flow teaches patience, calmly
Wearing away a rock, persistently
Creating a stream, skillfully.

Your tumbling waters full of grace,
Never are you in a race;
Carrying forth the secrets of time
In the roaring song of your chime.

In the molecules of your moist mist
Lies, quite proudly, nature's twist.
Day and night, unceasingly,
Waves rise and fall perpetually.

18

WORDS

Life is the embossed paper.
I, the pulsing, passionate poet,
Inscribe craftily,
Vibrating fingers flickering across pages.

Some days, a new masterpiece flitters;
Others, a distortion in blood-ink,
Burning dazzling white pages,
Painting between the lines.

Powerfully, eternally,
From the language of the heart,
Words spill onto the paper of life,
Transforming to a declaration, a truth.

Life is the embossed paper
Upon which we inscribe.
Meanings are made up
As the reader translate the language of feelings.

19

CHIMERA

Should I trust this feeling?
Will it lead me astray?
Should I tread upon this path
Or go the other way?

Is this an illusion?
Am I of sound mind?
Could this be a chimera?
Will I be left behind?

Should I plunge without a care
Into these muddied depths?
Will I be glad I did
Or forever wonder with regrets?

20

OCEAN

Your slippers laid on the edge of the beach.
On my periphery, I couldn't see your form.
I knew they were yours. I gave them to you.
It wasn't that long.
I sat on the edge of the lapping waves,
Staring at the horizon in a daze.
We had promised to meet on the water's edge.
I couldn't understand where you had gone instead.
Tears rolled off my cheeks unto the sand.
A seagull's cry shatters the repetitive sound.
Startled from my heart's reverie,
I felt the waters part, and you rose from the sea.
A beautiful image, you were in my sight,
Wading towards me with eyes so bright.
I have loved you all along.
Finally, we're together where we both belong.

21

GARDEN OF LOVE

Lying on the luscious green carpet,
Sprigs craftily tingled my neck.
The scents of your variety
Keeps my heart and mind in check.

Your beauty is natural;
No effort needed on your part.
You produce beauty and fragrance;
You are quite the poetic artist.

You take no benefit
From the garden or the land,
Naturally processing the nutrients,
The harsh weather you withstand.

The warmth of the sun aide your pace.
The rain adds its richness all around.
The space allows you to rise towards the sun.
Grateful, you abound.

You give life to Earth,
Exhaling what we inhale.
You are the embodiment of unconditional
Breathing, kindness without a fail.

22

BENEATH YOUR BEAUTIFUL

I want to look beneath your defined parts,
Underneath the layers of your constructed externality.
I want to undress your continuous exquisiteness.
I want to see you in your pure, natural rawness.
I want to see beneath your beautiful.

I want to peel back the layers of makeup,
Gently strip away the years of programming.
I want to take away all your certificates.
I want to see beyond your gates.
I want to see beneath your beautiful.

I want to peek into your artificial shell.
I know that walls are erected to protect
Fragile, beautiful heart.
I want to see beneath your defined parts.
I want to see beneath your beautiful.

I want to see your natural smile.
I want to feel your authentic delight.
I want to hear your joyous laughter ring.
I want to absorb all the traits you bring.
I want to see beneath your beautiful.

23

THE BOOK OF DESTINY

Once together, it's meant to be,
As written in the book of destiny.
Here we are, fulfilling this prophecy
In the heart of the cosmology.
Your love is alluring, exciting;
Mine is calm, inviting.
Our hearts pound in unison,
Like a giant cosmic explosion,
A starburst that was meant to be,
As written in the book of destiny.

24

HEART

The heart is a shrine,
A sacred home to love,
Ever pure and divine.

Trusting in its natural nature,
A warm place,
A quiet grace.

Perfuming with its fragrance
In rhythmic chants,
Ethereal, its radiance.

The mind takes over,
The heart loses its grip,
Obliterated by noisy clutter.

So, dance to love's chime.
Lose the mind and
Sing the tune of love divine.

25

MOON SUN

You are the sun; I am the moon.
Our love spans the expanse of the sky,
Existing for billions of years,
Never a hi; never a goodbye.

In the dawn and dusk,
I embrace your light.
Although not always seen by day,
I am as present as I am at dawn's sight.

We've known each other for eternity,
A love that is unbroken.
You know my every contour,
Although we've never spoken.

We are not selfish in our love.
We exist for others.
Our love is pure and authentic,
Full of surprises, full of wonder.

This love of ours is altruistic,
A cosmic mystery.
We are content being lovers,
Passing by each other silently.

26

LIFE

Man's self-created
boundaries
are not the sky's limits
of capabilities.

The winds hold
molecules of possibilities
that I will sail through
naturally.

I, the king of my destiny,
Believe in truth,
Not winning;
I play fair, never unkindly.

27

PERHAPS ONCE

Perhaps, once,
I will dare breathe
the same molecules you exhale
and tread my way into your heart
following love's muddy trail.

Perhaps, once,
I will dare luxuriate
in love's distinct fragrance
and allow its scent like Sandalwood
to imprint its tantalizing frangrance upon my heart.

Perhaps, once,
I will protest for and not against
a chance to taste love,
to experience a roaring lion
sitting beside a gentle dove.

Perhaps, once,
placing my doubts aside,
emerging from my shell,
I will give love a chance

to sound its trumpets
and every mouth our story will tell.

Perhaps, once,
I will surrender.
I will let my walls down,
And without restraints
in this sea of whispering desires,
allow myself to drown.

28

WOMAN

You are phenomenal.
You are the mother of creation.
You are strong and resilient.
You are the beginning of every individual.
Woman, you are exquisitely sculpted.

You are extra-terrestrial.
You are quite extraordinary.
You are the influence of the next generation.
You are passionate and kind
Woman, you are meticulously molded.

You are glamorously defined.
You are the never-ending stream of energy.
You go the extra mile,
Always wearing a smile.
Woman, you are intelligently refined.

You are grace defined.
You are artistry aligned.
You personify dignity.
You are the unconsciously sublime.
Woman, you are femininity rarefied.

29

LOVE'S FLOW

Love is patient.
Love is kind.
Her essence, most divine.
She seeks not to possess,
Dominate, or regress.
Filling cracks and voids,
Never selfish or devoid.

Pure, her energies ebb and flow,
Bringing streams of life aglow.
Never forcefully
But gently, quietly, subliminally,
She awaits an opening,
Allowing herself in.

Love teaches wisdom, not lessons.
We learn, expand, and grow,
Swimming in her everlasting stream.
Her waves, she glows,
Casting her radiance everywhere she flows.

30

HEARTBEAT

Each dew drop is a beautiful creation,
Touching Earth's toes in devotion.
Sands are alternate worlds,
Like ocean depths filled with pearls.

Flowers and trees are Earth's nostrils,
Breathing life, breathing promises.
At the heart of creation's dance
Is the heart of infinite radiance.

Each beating heart is a precious pearl,
Connected by vibrations across the world.
All of creation would not exist
Without beating hearts that coexists.

31

EYES

Destructive as tornado winds,
Spewing discrimination,
Spewing hate.

Fiery as a thousand suns,
Burning impressions,
Imaginations they create.

Conveying feelings,
x-rayed or radiance,
Is it as a sensory organ
Or a pulsing, conscious, life-force emission?

32

LOVE'S WORSHIP

I'm twirling in love.
Love's in the pores of my reality.
I'm surrounded by love's fragrance.
Love's perfume surrounds me drunkenly.

Intoxicatingly, I spin around.
In her embrace, she cushions me,
Cherishing and adoring me,
This pulsing feeling inside and around me.

I am inside the universe.
The universe is inside of me.
Love is worship and worship is love.
I'm in love and love is in me.

33

PATHS

Our paths crossed in time. Whether it was destiny or coincidence, I guess we'll never know. It's too brief to ask questions. Hours are all that is lent to us, and to fulfill an eternity of wait within this time would've been impossible. Had we not understood the preciousness of centuries apart, we could not have treasured this time together. This moment, however short, will have to last forever.

After centuries of parchment, your touch hydrates my soul. My love, let these moments in your arms sear a memory in my heart that will last forever. You are the dream of a lonely heart, the obsession of a desperate soul. These moments are the fulfillment my heart seeks that will have to last forever.

My love, please make it last more than a fleeting moment. Singe your love into my heart. Let this nectar of yours fill the oceans of longing and lifetimes of loneliness. Breathe me back to life. These treasured moments are ours, until our paths cross again.

34

DISTANCE

I have loved you from the time we were children, before we moved to different places and every day after that. Not once asking each other's permission, we surrendered willingly to love's mission, and wherever we find ourselves, I thought home was always back with each other.

The separation was heartrending, but bearable on the hope that one day, very soon, we'll be home again in each other's hearts.

Now I have returned, and my heart's afraid this love will be no more. The children we were, we are no more.

My fears are realized, adulthood came with rifts and barriers. This distance between us now, as we stand next to each other, is equivalent to galaxies apart. Time had taken its toll on our souls. The geographical distance and years apart had ripped our hearts asunder.

To own or to possess you, that I do not want. I will love you at the safe distance that's now between our hearts.

35

ENDLESS SEARCH

I ride the winds of destiny that blow your fragrance in my direction. Far and wide, searching eyes encompassed the Earth, ending upon that sudden glimpse of you. I know you are the one. How could you not be? My heart instantly lit aflame.

I fervently wish I never allow this light to be extinguished or this passion to burn out in the furnace of time. Should this moment end too soon, stand upon this mountain top and gently whisper my name.

Come, my love; apply thy heart's song upon my skin and let me absorb it into the cells of my being. Let us fill this void for lifetimes ahead. Today, let us not, our desires contain.

In this moment of passionate, euphoric rapture, I will carve thy name upon my heart. A love that spans eons and worlds and lifetimes has finally arrived. Hasten, my love. Hesitate not. A moment will be all we will share before lifetimes appear again and again.

36

PRINCE

You were the Prince of Persia. I hadn't a title to hold. I was dressed immaculately that night when our eyes clashed across the floor. You set off towards me in pursuit. I followed you to ballroom floor.

Slowly, we drank each other's gaze, filling the oasis in our hearts. I shivered when you pulled me closer than was reasonably respectable and moistened my parched lips, feeling peeved you'd hear my thunderous heart, but you leaned closer. Your breath warmed my ear. "Mine's also hammering away," you whispered. It was a reckless abandon as you pulled me through the door, finding myself in a moonlight-kissed garden, misted in dew and scented by roses blooms. You whispered how you wished the night would never end. End, it certainly did.

For up to 12, I was your princess, but that night is impressed in my heart forever. In that misted garden, I was a princess, adorned, adored, and loved, if only momentarily.

37

PROMISED NIGHT

The dew-kissed grass and fluorescent moon are my companions tonight while I await your arrival.

Walking sensuously along, barefooted, my heart's song goes, "This night was promised to me." It's what I have fervently looked forward to – our meeting along the edge of the ocean.

I spun around in anticipation at our rendezvous, my heart fluttering like the wings of a butterfly and the wind whipping my tresses across my face. My gait was light and innocent, dancing a happy song.

I had every right, as it was our night, this night that was promised to me.

38

FLEETINGLY

You arrived like a windblown Atlantic storm, shaking my life to its core.

We shared our life's dream in a moment – to travel the world, wild and free, and swim in every deep blue sea,

but your presence in my heart lasted only fleetingly.

Every face I behold, I'm searching for yours, for your sultry smile, your refined elegance, and the twinkle in your golden flecks. Your imprints have been molded in my heart,

but your presence in my heart lasted only fleetingly.

In love's pure floating euphoric state, I never engaged the mind. I trusted you implicitly,

but your presence in my heart lasted only fleetingly.

I searched for you endlessly after you disappeared into cyberspace. Every coroner of the media scene, you were unknown, but I will continue to scan across the globe despite

your presence in my heart that lasted only fleetingly.

39

INFERNO

Today is the cremation of a bond that had gone sour ages ago. I had walked away, so many times before in my mind, returning through emotional enmeshed webs, grappling me unconsciously, but today, today I choose me.

Standing among the rubble, I feel neither sorrow nor joy. Free at last, I am, as the smoke rises from the ashes. I am so much wiser than when I held your hand many moons ago, longing to finally return after this tedious trail.

Maybe, in the molecular structure of time, you were never meant to be mine nor I yours, for I truly believe that a happy ending was ours to grasp, just not beside each other.

40

RAIN

The thirsty earth beckons you. "Come." Patter, patter, raindrops scatter, bringing to life the parched, arid land. Your landing upon the rooftops is quite a thunderous sound, although you are soundless in your pace.

Your arrival is refreshing, energizing, and sparkling, bringing a drop of new life to all without discrimination. Your monsoons delayed will create despair. Your molecules hold the trace of life.

Raindrops, you are a necessity. The thirsty earth beckons you. "Come."

41

STORY OF LOVE'S WAITING

It has been an era of waiting. The time stretches on infinitely.

The wait is torturous; slow.

The sky never really touches the sea, and the sun laughingly tries to reach the ocean. Our meeting has become like this, almost impossible, one of endless anticipation where years are turned into centuries and I'm counting each grain in the sands of time.

The wait is torturous; slow.

I never asked for much, just a meeting of our hearts, fulfilling a promise, and while each day brings that promise closer, the wait is still torturous; slow.

42

FOREST

On the dried leaves and twigs of the forest floor, I slept. I had not a clue of how long it had been. A few hours, a few years, maybe? Birds chirped. Monkeys squealed. Bees buzzed, yet I remained, dreamlessly sleeping, waking only to a whispering sound like a falling leaf. "Arise, my love. It's time to leave."

With arms outstretched and eyes still closed, I was lifted into unfamiliar arms. My eyes darted opened in a shock to stare into the warm autumn sun. Your breath rustled my hair and tickled my nose. "Who are you?" escaped a hoarse whisper. "I've come but to take you home, dear one. The path had been long and winding. Years have passed since that day you wandered away and fell asleep. Now, today, just seeing your eyelids flutter, I feel you are already home."

43

AGRA

On the steps at Agra, I stood, nostalgia bubbling up inside.
There was a sense of familiarity, like I had been here before.
I traced the intricately carved marble design reverently. An
electric shock ran up my arms, tugging
at my heart's chambers. A nagging feeling of being here years
before swept across my mind. How could that have been, as
this was my very first, once-in-a-lifetime visit to Agra?

I entered the door of this adored beauty, my first steps met
with flooding memories. I could see the king, dismayed at
losing his beautiful one. Had I been there, or had I been loved
like that? Had I also known a love so pure, a love so strong
that standing at the Taj's steps made me feel as if I had
carved my name on its marble floor eras before?

44

SHELL

I was invisible because I was taught to be, and so I stayed where I was unseen and unheard. At the sign of danger, I pulled right in and curled into a ball. Then, I bought into your game of trying hard to become better than you, to become stronger than you, giving up my innate abilities to imitate your manly ones. All it took was for me to recognize what I was really made of – strength and creativity, vulnerability and femininity. I didn't need to be another you. No one, I hope, is another you.

45

FEELINGS

The heart hath not a clue of wickedness. It lived in the molten, golden sea of pure, flowing emotions. Through my cluttered mind, I allowed tinges of grey to enter unsuspectingly, silently flowing through my blood and entering my heart's reservoir.

Like a subtle, silent cat burglar, distaste and disdain seeped in through the windows of my heart, sweeping pureness under the mind's sea. I listened not to my heart's harmonic frequencies as the mind now loudly beats the drums to illusion's song whilst I wearily trudged on.

I craved the innocence I once possessed, the rare beauty of my intuitive heart. Good cheer and immense love were once my distinct traits before I allowed the grey to enter. May I somehow be able to clear the clutter and allow the flow of that molten, golden sea of pure emotions I was a home to once?

46

SEA

When I am with the sea, there is no pretense. Here I can be who I want to be and let down my hair. Immersing in her warm depths, she ensconces and surrounds me. Ripples of joy seep into the cells of my being. I care not about the next minute. It is just the warm, accommodating, dark ripples and me. In this moment, life is meant to be lived embracing the sea's bestowing generosity and let my soul fly free.

47

LOVE

Love accepts neither an invitation nor does it make reservations, arriving instead, like the cool waters of the ocean or that of raging winds, sweeping you off your feet. Sometimes, it soundlessly sneaks in and surprises you with a bunch of fragrant roses. Sometimes, it echoes off the rooftops. Other times, it soars like an eagle that you want to evade, gliding speedily towards you.

Love is boundless and sees no difficulties. It has no hidden agenda. It's spontaneous. Love has not a path; the journey is a wonder. It has no direction. Wherever the winds blow, you will find this pure feeling. Opening like the bud of a baby rose, spreading its fragrance and beauty on every face, in every heart, love is the beloved and you are the lover. Enter thou into infinite union.

48

RELATIONSHIPS OF THE HEART

Shrouded in a veil, her eyes are shy and benign. Her gaze lowered, anticipating this meeting. The garden was misty and the moon's pale glow lighted the path. The scents from chamomile and jasmine tingled her senses. She sat on the wooden bench, crossing and uncrossing her legs a hundred times.

Her eyes darted to the path as she heard a twig crunch, her heart dancing in her chest as she stood and spun around. In his arms she fell, tripping on the hem of her gown. Strong arms reached and clasped her close to him. She could hear his heart hammering in unison with hers, intoxicated. The light in his eyes made her heart race even faster. A pearl of love dropped from her eyes and he gently touched her cheek. He whispered, barely a sound, "Why did you wait so long for your heart's message to be sound?"

She filled the centuries of longing, drinking in his gaze. The memory of this love's fragrance perfumed her soul, and the remembrance of this love was what made life tolerable for centuries gone. This meeting had been planned for centuries. Oh, the wait! This night was all they were allowed for centuries to come. A love so innocent, asking for nothing except the moments like these that are lent, the chance of love fusing a relationship of hearts.

49

DREAMER

I woke up this morning to everything racing in the opposite direction. It felt surreal. I was floating in the clouds of sleepy awareness. Others thought it was a reality and expected it to last forever. Minds broken, they rouse sleepily, barley a few, asking the way through the jungles of mirages. Some said, "Ridiculous!" or "We are floating in space!"

He said, "Within!" And whilst others kept dreaming, scaling the clouds of illusions, he walked away, headed the other direction.

50

MEETING

Our departure was many moons ago. Each night, I arrive at our meeting place, sitting on our favorite rock, resting my hand on your seat that's still warm in my heart. I stare at the horizon and the reflection of the moon's light, glowing on the rising waves, lost in reverie of this love that was witnessed by the sand and the sea. Both our lives were filled with its history.

When we were at this meeting place, words were never needed to explain the heart's need. In the silence, we became lovers of the night. This night, I fervently wished you were here.

There you are, bathed in the pale moonlight. I blinked rapidly at this sight. Adonis, a God, who had arrived silently, just to be with me on this night, pulled me into his arms, wordlessly. Love, warm and gentle, offered a cool solace.

In the solitude of the subtle moonlight, this meeting took place.

51

ANCIENT LOVE

At the pyramid of Giza, I stood, reminiscing at this fascinating relic, this period of history, silently assuming its origins. I felt a piercing gaze and glanced about. You were standing in a room, watching the hieroglyphics. I stood admiring the tomb of the king. As our eyes locked, you walked across the gap of the room, as though our eyes invited each other. Your dark gaze, mysterious as well as familiar, pulled at my heart's strings, loosening all knots. Your breath was warm, brushing my cheeks and stirring my hair. Although you were standing afar, the fiery depths of your gaze drowned lifetimes of a burning desire I did not know I had, and now, this moment, is recorded on these walls at Giza as a love saga.

52

STAR LOVER

Your message arrived like meteor particles amidst the noise of clambering minds and screeching tires. I had sent so many messages to you that I thought went unheard and I sang love songs that I hoped, like a timeless vapor, would rise to reach your heart. I know now that you had received them and that love just arrives in its own time.

I jolted in shock on receipt of your heart's reply, bursting in ecstatic joy. The crashing sound of your love's arrival on Earth's plane engulfed me, hugging my heart close to yours in a tranquil moment. I lived for that day of union with you, my star lover.

53

CARIBBEAN

Like the cool waters of the Caribbean Sea,
You came floating towards me,
Sudden and surprising,
Winded, heart beating.
I recognized your gaze and gait;
Couldn't remember where we had met.
Staring across the pavilion,
Heart racing nine to a million,
Who are you, one with such grace?
I don't know you, but that gaze
Went to the depths of my soul's maze.
It has been a long, winding chase.
Heart thundering, pupils dilated,
Body shivering, heart tilted,
I drowned in those eyes staring back at me,
Eyes as blue as the Caribbean Sea.

54

SECRETS

She masked her true feelings through lowered lashes and half-smiles, letting none close enough, lest they view her deep, dark, ever-present secrets, and while she wore five layers of an impenetrable mask, under her veil was an innocent heart scared of being undone. She surrounded herself with self-worth and integrity and wore a coat of outer responsibility, afraid of being ridiculed and hurt, but you were not going to let that stop you from reaching her heart and making your home there.

You tapped her shoulders, and she spun around, piercing her soul like magnetic resonance. She lowered her frightened gaze, shielding behind the impenetrable veneer, hands trembling, flustered, and feelings ricocheting against her heart's walls. Skittishly lifting her eyes, losing herself in your poignant expression, she shook her head as if grasping at sanity. After a lifetime of an imprisoned heart, she yearned to trust your warm, blue gaze. She yearned to, just this one time, trust her heart's lead and lift her mask.
Your heart whispered, "You loved all of me."

56

GAZING

We held each other's hands, staring out at the horizon, the huge orange sun touching the ocean. A light wind whipped my hair across my face as I turned to soak in your contours. The heart sang a new rhythm that matched yours, and I couldn't take my gaze away from this soul-locking embrace of our eyes. I had searched for you in all the corners of the Earth without a clue that you'd ever belong to me. I always felt that you were destiny's child, and so, at that moment, I was truly delighted that you were beside me. Your gaze disclosed that you had absolved all previous encounters and will now be my absolution.

57

LOVE'S SILENT FIELDS

Chatter is a fool's pursuit to hide pain. I wish only for your silence. Placing my palm in yours, silently, we walked out into the fields of love that tantalized our senses. Dazzled by the beauty of the roses, you pointed to the thorns. I instantly discerned. Roses were useless without the thorns, the same way love would not be felt had there been no previous prick. The skilled gardener knew the secrets all along but remained silent, allowing us to get pricked, awakening this fervor in love's potent gardens. He beckons to the wailing heart, silently, "Enter, thou lover, at your own risk." Heeding the fragrant call of love's lure, silently, we walk into its fields.

58

ACCEPTANCE

The conditioned identity wants to judge and hold you responsible for its heart's distress. I just want to sit in the garden of eternal love and await thee, solemnly. Each precious flower belongs to the bouquet. I am also a decoration in the garden of love. A dry twig, the grass, a leaf, and a rose, together they beautify the garden, each giving no competition, never discrimination.

So, why can't I adopt the pace of nature's love divine, for I also happen to be a decoration in its garden? In this pace, I await you to smell the fragrance of a love, pure and innocent, a love that has survived turmoil, distance, and separation, a love that now awaits communion and the decoration of its own garden.

59

DESERT OF THE HEART

Like the molecules of breeze from the Saharan Desert, you appeared in the dry, arid region of my heart. It had been a harsh season of enduring loneliness and darkness in your absence. Your appearance was a dew drop in the early morning where none had ever been seen before, a sight most refreshing.

Your warmth, I couldn't shake off. My eyes were glued to yours as we searched the souls of each other. Oh, my love, 'twas the sweetest moment to recognize your heart and mine entwined as we stared at the infinite potential of this eternal love that binds our hearts together, irrespective of time, space, or distance. Sealing this solemn promise of our forever love was the wind, the sky, and Earth, acting as witnesses. Come closer, my love. Let our hearts unite, combine, synthesize, and bask in the freedom to be with each other for just this time.

60

REFUGE

I hid my face as you passed, refusing to acknowledge my need for you. I wanted to stand alone, as I did for the thousands of nights you weren't there.

Gently, you knocked, for never have you been one to enter uninvited. I knelt in a corner, hiding behind a veil of resistance. Perhaps I should let this consuming fire take control of me. Perhaps it's time I do.

As our eyes met, all my hesitancy and worries vanished. I sank into rapturous indulgence, my hunger leaving with the thousands of nights spent not having you there with me.

In you, alone, my refuge was found.

61

MATTERS OF THE HEART

All that really matters is what's felt by the heart – the joys and exhilaration, the laughter that rises from deep within, waking up beside you to the morning sun and dawn's beautiful warm gift of rays promising a day full of fun.

All that really matters is what's felt by the heart – the wonder of nature, scaling eyes, searching feet, the shade of trees, the work of bees, and a life of endless possibilities.

All that really matters is what's felt by the heart – the taste of a great romance, the dance of our lips, deep and profound love stories, holding your hand, and creating treasured memories.

62

ENIGMA

Standing in your courtyard feeling hesitant in the amassed wealth, I am just a peasant. My eyes rested longingly on you. You were dressed in an elegant robe, sitting on your golden throne.

I turned to walk away, thinking, "I'm delusional entering here." Hesitantly, I spun around at the call of my name. "I'm sure I heard my name!" There you were, in your kingly robe and jeweled crown. My eyes fluttered like a butterfly's wings. There I was, in the arms of the king. You touched my face. Your forehead had a worried crease. Wearily, my gaze met yours, mystified, surprised, and perplexed. Yours was beautifully decorated with pearls of love.

63

UNDONE

Like the Indian monsoon, our love down poured from melancholic dark clouds. Turbulent pain erupted into a howling thunder. My pierced heart had inscribed your name, drenching itself in a love, completely undone, never seeking my consent to do so, never seeking my consent at all when it came to you.

Nights alone, crumpled into a ball, weeping in the language of quiet, I understood that sometimes love doesn't always love us back. Powerful is the strength of unrequited love, perhaps the only bond that is never shared, but did I dare? It was unthinkable not to. I faltered on its slippery slopes and fell headlong into the waiting arms of my own suffering.

Now I write of a fragile love, lost before it even became mine, the pain visible only to the ones who have loved and lost the love they never got. Now my laughter has become plastic, and my smile, pasted. I am a lover, completely undone.

64

SILENCE

In silence lies the sleeping beauty, waiting, envisaging her dreams realized. For creation, sustainability, and explored anonymity, pure silence is needed; she knows. Her true capabilities float to the surface, pulled by gravity of this silence. She flows as if in a dream, unearthly, ethereal, and they all want to possess her; she knows. It's the illusion of this falsity that they have esteemed to be real. Her wisdom is her shield, protecting her from the unreal. She desires for each to arise and be pulled by the gravity of this silence.

65

TIME TRAVEL

We sailed through the timeless opening, landing in a world so gorgeously wealthy. We were beckoned to enter separate rooms where I was redressed. The robes were pure silk, embellished with beautiful jewels and golden threads. The pearls and rubies glistened under the lighted ceiling. Diamonds decorated the ceiling and all around. The falling light made the room appear like a magical white kingdom.

My hair was brushed gently and decorated with emeralds. I immediately glided towards the mirror in the far end to behold my reflection of skin so porcelain smooth, hair, a long glistening silk garment covering my back, and eyes that burned like stars in the inky night.

The objects were spectacularly unique, reeking of wealth, class, and originality. Attending to me were beautifully dressed fairies. They beckoned forward, sprinkling scented roses. They were mistaken. I was not royal. I... I glided along a decorated balustrade into a room of immaculately dressed others who ushered me to the front. The front row parted, alas, as my glance lifted. Golden thrones were just ahead where you were already seated. You beckoned me. "Come!

We'd been waiting." As the ceremony began, "The coronation of the emperor and the empress" was whispered by the children.

In some past life, I must've been here. Surely, we were here. We looked at each other and imprinted this royal memory on our hearts' eternal seal, for soon we were to leave, and this memory will be all that we'd be allowed to take on our time travel.

66

DESIRE

Longing rips my restless mind to shreds, tearing the cells of my soul apart. The heart echoes a sad note, wrapped in yearning by the forces of desires. I sit and beckon the stars to send you to me. You, the inimitable lover, my heart is creating. It paints your form in the galaxies, writing your name in the heart of the universe, infusing you with life. Yours is a love conceived in the womb of my heart. My very existence is intertwined in yours. How will you not become a reality? The forces of desires will infuse you with life, bringing you to actuality.

67

MISSION ACCOMPLISHED

Gnarled hands reached for her
With the desire to possess,
Grappling at her body,
The external brilliance.

She is a mirage,
A shadow of their illusory mind.
Driven by a fiery need,
They are blindfolded to its after-effects.

Casting a razor-sharp beam,
Her gaze-smothered recognition
Piercing their darkness
With the beams of her wand.

The glowing embers still faintly lit,
A long-needed awakening.
Walking away, she was a smiling.
"Mission accomplished."

68

PULSING DARKNESS

Lying on the floor in fetal posture, swishing leaves scatter the silence seeking reprieve from tumultous emotions. The inky blackness draped the scattered diamonds in the sky, wishing to slip into the waiting arms of emptiness. Your resonating call has left this fragile heart stupified, afraid, and uncertain of the response it must give, if any is needed at all.

Should I slide over the edge of uncertainty, trusting inbred wisdom? Should I taste the desires from the throbbing universe ? Dare I plunge for once, live and sail freely, mindlessly? Should I surrender to the pulsing darkness draping the diamond sky, bridging the gap of reality, floating on a star in the inky night?

69

UNINVITED

To walk through gates where you are not welcome is quite the bold thing to do. You beheld with much curiosity and stepped through, not caring much about the lurking dangers. Thorns paved the way, a necessary nutrient for new saplings.

Uninvited, you walked in, magnetically pulled of your own accord like a pin surrendering to the pull of a magnet, the potent fragrance of my roses. It is said that opposites attract. Maybe that's why roses and thorns are companions forever. Their beauty hides in the thorn's nutritive quality and hardly ever found solo. Should you not have known?

You were never invited into my garden. You came of your own accord. Startled by a crunching twig, you looked up and beheld the gardener, shrouded by the shades of a huge bough. There was no escaping unhurt. Her prick was an addictive nutrient, once and you can no longer break free. You walked in, uninvited, and now you're eternally bonded for infinity by your uncontrollable curiosity.

See, to walk through gates where you're not welcome is quite the bold thing to do, and I probably would not have dared if I were you.

70

ECLIPSE

Restlessly tossing, turning,
A cold and sleepless night,
Shrouded by darkness,
The veil of the lonely light.

Under the skin of the pulsing universe,
A dark and empty space,
Are desires, wild and tame,
Hidden in a crammed briefcase.

Your absence pulls on
The strings of my heart's notes.
My pain is hidden underneath,
Multiple padded coats.

Your presence, innocent and pure,
Leaves an accute ache,
A lingering frangrance,
Sleepless nights in its wake.

I desire you,
Just as much as you do me,
But I am a thorn with prickly sides.
My exitence is just such, you see.

The art of leaving, I've mastered before.
With one's heart, I cannot play.
This is my gentle withdrawal,
Not wishing harm your way.

71

WHISPERING MOON

Her rehearsed steps resonate with the wind.
She is a silver orb dancing on the heart of the night sky,
Glowing brighter than her cosmic friends,
Yet ever humble and shy.

She hides mysteries around her edges,
Brings warmth to humid hearts,
Whispers her vulnerability, showing her flaws,
Leaving an ache for more when she desparts.

72

DESIRE

Curled, restless, haunted in solitude,
My heart's melancholic call echoes,
"Mi Amor,
Why are you hiding in the shadows?"

My mind has been shredded,
My soul's cells ripped apart,
Longing, yearning,
Great is the ache of my heart.

For decades, I beckoned the stars,
"Do send him to me."
The inimitable lover my heart's been creating,
The one custom-made for me.

It paints his form in the galaxies,
Carving the letters of his name,
Infusing him with life,
His arrival, I proclaim.

A love conceived in the womb of my heart;
My very existence intertwined in his.
Is he a reality,
Or a dream born from delusion, a fantasy?